COME ALIVE TO HER HEART

A Challenge for Married Men on Emotional Connecting

BRUCE LENGEMAN

SECOND EDITION

ISBN: 978-1-946466-98-3

Library of Congress Control Number: 2020915876

Published by

Certa PUBLISHING

3741 Linden Avenue SE | Grand Rapids, MI 49548

Printed in the United States

Dedication

Who else could I dedicate this book to other than Ruthie, who for 44 years has taught me many of the principles you are about to read. She has had supernatural patience with all the things I had to learn. I love you!

Acknowledgments

Thanks to my daughter and son-in-law, Krystal and Ryan McFadden, who edited and gave me tips that improved this book. Thanks also to my good friend Brian Fulmer, who introduced me to Grammerly—a grueling process. He also suggested Sarah Sauder with Partnership Publications who did all my formatting, and like she always does, offered amazing suggestions on how to improve the book—thank you!

And a hearty thanks always goes to the "gems" at Certa Publishing, which could be accurately named *Serving Publishing*, because that's what they do—care and serve!

Table of Contents

Introduction

The book you are about to read is flawed.

I struggled writing a book on this subject because of the illusive mystery of manhood. I find it both complex and, at times, undesirable to try to put "shoulds" on men—to pull back on their testosteronal leash. At times I bristled when my wife, Ruthie, would do that to me! Yet, I know many, if not most, men's leashes need tugged into the reality of the need for emotional connecting in marriage.

In general, men have "spikes" in their nature that women don't have. And though this book is primarily about the needs of women, I acknowledge that we men have distinct needs too, though most of them won't be addressed in this book. There was a season a decade or two ago when it seemed as if so many of the books chided men for their relational failures. A friend of mine said he was tired of male-bashing books. I will have failed in my efforts if this book leaves you with a bad-boy impression. I am diligent to choose my words wisely to avoid unnecessary condemnation directed at the male species.

So, in writing this, in attempting to be true and balanced, while keeping this book short and to the point, I may miss a peripheral point that may be a significant factor in your marriage experience.

Please understand, that when I say this book is flawed, I don't mean that what I have written may not be true—I know it to be true. But there may be MORE truth that this document will not address. And I will leave that up to you and God to figure out together!

Having said that, I invite all married men to *Come Alive to Her Heart!*

CHAPTER 1

What Women Need, What Men Have to Give

Lisa wept as she talked to Ruthie about her hurting heart—hurting because her husband had little interest in conversation with her, didn't share with her his inner feelings, and only lent a brief ear to the things she needed to talk about. Lisa represents many women—too many—who are aching for their husbands to connect to their hearts.

It's not only the lack of verbal connection that causes a woman to ache emotionally for something more from her husband, it may be a plethora of things. Things such as not valuing her opinions and viewpoints, not making her feel beautiful, him putting other people or endeavors ahead of her, and more, all could feel like emotional violations.

Unfortunately, many women who are hurting in their marriage have embraced a survival technique—stuff your feelings and survive with what you got! I'm convinced, though, that God has a better plan for marriage.

Of course, men aren't all to blame. A woman may be demanding, emotionally needy in an unhealthy way, and so forth. I acknowledge that. But in this book we are primarily addressing what men can do to enliven their marriage and nurture a relational culture that supports healthy emotions for both the husband and the wife.

I was tempted to begin this book with a poem I wrote, "You're a Princess," because it says everything I want to say. But I perceived that some teaching needed to happen before I dropped the poem on you at the end. Don't cheat. There are some things you need to learn first.

You see, I think one of the most important lessons we need to teach our sons is how to hold, heal, and protect the heart of a woman. If this were a part of our culture, there would be fewer marriage problems, less pornography, and more women living emotionally healthy lives. But, alas, how many men can say that they were taught as sons how to support a woman's heart?

Though Ruthie and I never went through a bad season in our marriage, I am still learning how to better tap into Ruthie's heart. I could tell a thousand stories of times I missed her heart—like trying to shoot the bull's eye with an arrow and missing the target altogether. Perhaps I could more accurately say that there were times I sabotaged her heart—unintentionally. And I stress that I did it unintentionally.

Why Am I Writing about This?

I am on a journey to revive the dignity of manhood that our culture has consistently attempted to poison. Men need to be taught how to be real men, not the weak, fragile, palatable, safe, and compliant models the world has defined for maleness.

I am constantly pulling bits and pieces of what true manhood looks like from military commanders, world leaders, influential missionaries, business icons—traits I was never taught by this world or the church. I assure you that my discourse in this book is not meant to diminish the tenacity of maleness. But in all my observations I have found out indisputably that true maleness is both steel and velvet, and men who fail to develop the God-like sensitive, intimate capacity of their heart will have failed to discover the true meaning of manhood.

I have wanted to write this book for a long time because of how often we hear of couples struggling with unfulfilled emotions. The problem is not just with men, but women too. But in the counseling room we have had to address the lack of romantic intimacy far more often with men than with women. I'm not pointing fingers at any man or men in general, but I do want to influence and challenge men who possess a desire to learn how to be a more emotionally connected husband. If you are a husband, I want to help you if your emotional insensitivity is wounding your wife—I want to give you some advice on how to improve your marriage and nurture your wife's heart!

Is Marriage All about Romance?

I am fully aware that the success in marriage can't be gauged by a thermometer of emotional fulfillment. Marriage is much more. Marriage is a picture of God's relationship with His people. Marriage is a wonderful institution that equips two people to grow closer to God, and to become better at being themselves. As I write this, Ruthie and I are preparing for a marriage conference we are teaching this coming weekend. The theme of this conference centers around the truth that success in marriage is more about personal holiness, maturity, and strong character than it is about emotional fulfillment.

Nevertheless...

Though success in marriage is more than emotional fulfillment, I will not diminish the importance of married people diligently growing in the knowledge of what fulfills their partner emotionally. Affairs begin with people emotionally unfulfilled in their marriage seeking to fill voids that ought to be filled in marriage. Men, what I am about to say may infringe on your personal comfort zones, and even your false perception of maleness, but please listen to me and consider if what I'm about to address applies to you. I am not attempting to feminize you or make you touchey-feeley. I am calling you to your privilege of nurturing an emotionally healthy wife.

In my opinion, the vacuum of male intimacy is magnified in our society, one that nurtures unhealthy, self-centered living. This self-focus is evident even among those who perceive themselves committed to Jesus. Like never before men are NOT being taught that it is a privilege to protect women—even their emotions. And to top it off, to a large degree our present culture has caved to twisted political attempts to erase the wonderfulness of male authority that is so vital for a woman's heart!

Before We Get Going

I finished the manuscript of the book you are reading and sent it over to a friend to edit. Then, this morning, I was motivated to add one more paragraph here, at the beginning. There are reasons why the Bible refers to God in masculine terminology, which I won't address here. But God is the embodiment of NOT just male qualities—the essence of testosterone, but, in terms of characteristics, He emanates every bit as much female as male. If this were not the case, women would be a lesser species. He is steel, and He is velvet. He is soft and sensitive. He is strong and tenacious. He perpetuates intimacy with all those in relationship with Him. He is the Author and Finisher of womanhood, and the same with maleness. I am not feminizing God. I am simply saying that He is *All in All.* The glory of this is when a husband and a wife find that sweet spot of oneness, they portray a beautiful picture of God to the world.

CHAPTER 2

Mikah's Confession and What That Evoked

ACTS, the church I attend, hosts an epic annual, winter men's retreat—Friday through Sunday noon. Lots of guys who don't attend ACTS join the event, and a host of teens. The DNA of the event doesn't include a lot of teaching sessions. The bulk of the time is relational connecting—on the comfy rockers, in the gym, shooting clay pigeons. This year our special speaker was Keith Blank—the perfect choice for a men's retreat!

Saturday night was no less than awesome. Dan led the worship portion. We had six guitars, two ukuleles, three percussions. The three hours of organic unpracticed worship and an anointed message by Keith opened the door to an evening of spontaneous interaction of men praying for each other and sharing challenges at the mic. At one point all the men gathered around the teens and prayed life and destiny into them.

The platform of free-sharing was set. On Sunday morning Keith invited anyone to come forward to tell what God was putting His finger on in their heart this weekend. Mikah boldly came forward. Passionately he shared the challenging journey he was having connecting emotionally with his wife. They had been married less than five years.

Keith's idea was to surround and pray for those bold enough to come forward. But instead of praying for *just* Mikah, Keith sensed that several of the guys resonated with Mikah. He invited them forward to be prayed for also.

Then Keith asked if I would come forward and pray over the men. I didn't count how many men came forward, but it was more than I would have expected. As I prayed, there were apparent tears in the eyes of guys who earnestly wanted to know how to connect in a wholesome way with their wives, but felt crippled to do it well. The men who came forward because of their DIS-connect with their wives did not lack the desire to do so, but for most of them, an inner crippling hindered their needed emotional bonding. And for some of the guys, it was a sadness—they wanted to fulfill their wives, but they were missing the bull's-eye in their efforts.

Thankfully, they cared. That incident reminded me that the need to teach men how to connect heart-to-heart with their wives is more significant than what appears on the surface.

A bit later I will tell you what I prayed over those men that day, but first let me make a few comments.

Physically Present—Emotionally Absent

One day I picked up a book my wife, Ruthie, was reading by Lysa Terkurst, *Uninvited*. She, two of our daughters, and a couple of friends were using it for a book discussion on Tuesday nights. In chapter two I saw these words highlighted:

"When a man is physically present but emotionally absent, a girl's heart can feel quite hollow and helpless."

What I'm about to share with you comes from more hours counseling marriages than Road Runner clocked running from Wiley Coyote. It is also the result of many years of experience as a pastor, walking with friends, and, perhaps, mostly from wisdom gained from my own marriage.

CHAPTER 3

Three Categories of Disconnect

There are three categories of men who have intimacy disconnects:

1. **Men with blocks to intimacy.** These men have mental and/or emotional blocks to intimacy. In this category are men who have had over-nurturing or dominant mothers, or they have been wounded by a woman—perhaps a girlfriend, a female teacher, or even experienced sexual abuse from a woman. Men in this category need a measure of inner healing to release their heart.
2. **Men who never learned about intimacy.** Men who grew up where intimacy was never modeled, taught, or intimacy was modeled as weak or feminine may think it is silly for a woman to be so needy. As a result, he may withhold from his wife the emotion she needs because HE doesn't need that kind of emotional connection. Men in this category need to see the intimate nature of God and learn how much women need the nurturing heart of a man. It's the way God made women.
3. **Men who don't know the differences.** These are men who

don't have the issues of the first two categories, but they happen to be normal men who simply don't understand how women are different from men. It also could be they don't understand how their wife's personality profile or love language differs from his. All men are in this category at some point. We simply need to go through the process of learning how women tick, and the best teachers are our wives themselves.

The book you are reading is not a male-bashing teaching, nor is it one of those "let's feminize men" discourses. So, (please, guys, read to the end) because I am going to attempt to present a stable, balanced view, while at the same time instructing and challenging you to connect emotionally in a deeper way with your wife.

I want to say here that a man who fails to learn to connect with the emotional needs of his wife is unequipped for a long-lasting, thriving marriage. You can blame your wife's delicate emotions or her needy-bleedy heart all you want, but learning how to satisfy the emotional needs of your wife is not optional if you want a great marriage AND a great family!

Clueless

Almost all men, perhaps all men, myself included (as you will see), have to overcome a measure of cluelessness when it comes to living with a woman. Cluelessness defined: a lack of understanding of female needs that differ from men's.

But honestly, multitudes of men are creating chaos in

their marriages because of extreme cluelessness. Difficulty understanding women is nothing to be ashamed of. I am merely pointing out that sometimes we men didn't come out of our mother's womb with an innate understanding of how to meet the emotional needs of women—needs that in many ways significantly and vastly differ from ours.

Many years ago, a friend gave me a book that helped me tremendously—*Discovering the Mind of a Woman* by Ken Nair. When Ruthie and I were in a setting where the book came up in conversation, I would jokingly say, "The pages are blank!" She would counter-attack by saying, "It's a multi-volume set." Alas, she was right. Men think women are complex. But women think men are complex too. So, how do we discover places of disconnect between the mind and heart of a woman and the mind and heart of a man?

Clueless or Careless?

Yes, most, if not all men, are clueless to varying degrees, but some men are careless—care-less—they don't care that they are clueless. In this category are men who are not pursuing a culture of oneness with their wives—they only want what they want. They want to control for their own satisfaction. Another word for *care-less-ness* is *narcissism*—deep-rooted selfish living. If you are a narcissist you won't get much out of reading this book, unless by reading this you realize that you are a narcissist and choose to change.

Robbie and Danielle

Robbie is someone I know who knows how to make things work. He is one of a broad category of men who are gifted in making things happen, whether in ministry, humanitarian work, or making money. What I have observed in my involvement with them is that Robbie listens to Danielle when he thinks he can benefit from her opinion, but his style is to do what he wants to do even when it violates Danielle's values. Both she and he seem very blinded by success, and therefore Danielle justifies stuffing her feelings, believing that she is inadequate compared to Robbie. So what's wrong with that? The issue is, though a measure of apparent success is happening, many things pertaining to the Kingdom of God aren't. Robbie's narcissism works, but many virtues and values are discarded along the way.

I believe both Robbie and Danielle love God and are attempting to do good, but my guess is that somewhere along the way, God will intervene with a plan designed to bring Robbie and Danielle into a place where they give full control of their lives to God.

Not all care-less-ness is narcissism. But as you are reading this section, do some inner reflection: ask yourself if there are places you don't care to please your wife. If there are places like this, pause now and give control of those things back to God.

CHAPTER 4

Two Become One? Are You Kidding?

When I officiated the wedding of Andrea and Alastair, my youngest daughter and son-in-law, I said this:

"Andrea and Alastair, when I say, 'Now I pronounce you husband and wife', in the sight of God you are ONE. The two become one—legally, officially, spiritually, you are ONE in God's eyes positionally. That is the easy part."

The Hard Part

"Now you must become one experientially in the way you live, and that is the greatest challenge in maintaining a fruitful marriage. But more than that—much more—this is the blessing and privilege of marriage—by becoming one experientially, you both better yourselves and create a greater opportunity for fruitfulness."

I continued, "This process of becoming one experientially will NOT take humility to accomplish."

Pause for Reflection

"Andrea and Alastair, it will take BRUTAL humility. Death

to self-centeredness. You must move from independence to interdependence, never giving up your unique design, but blending as a new creation."

Lopsided Living

When you are single, you have the grace of God to be single, but when you are married, you don't have the grace to live as a single person. People who carry their independent single-ness into marriage are living lopsided. *Two becoming one* means just that—change and adapt. I repeat, one's independence must become interdependence.

What "Two Become One" Does NOT Mean

Becoming "one" doesn't mean that you and she water down or compromise your original design. Yes, there must be give-and-take in any relationship, but becoming one means that you, together, operate as one unit. She has her strengths and gifts, and you have yours. Put them together, celebrate your differences, and learn to flow with each other to become a powerful "unit," maximizing life together. Be careful not to try to change something in your spouse that was not meant to be changed!

The Problem

Sometimes the emotional disconnect stems from men reserving the right to be male, expecting his wife to undergird his maleness while failing to understand and support the femaleness of his wife. The result: women emotionally unfulfilled at different levels, while men are content with the way things are.

The couples we have counseled who relate to the above scenario do not necessarily always have a bad marriage. Simply, the wife feels not being taken care of emotionally, and sometimes even starves to hear the endearments from her husband that fuel her heart. It may simply be that a husband is unaware that God made women with strong emotional connectors for a good—no, great—reason. For the most part, your wife needs to hear sincerely that you love her, why you love her, and why she is valuable to you and the world. And she needs to see it demonstrated.

CHAPTER 5

Disclaimers and What Women Say

A Few Things to Clarify

1. Men can be emotionally unfulfilled in a relationship, too, because women also have detachment issues. I do not deny that. I am primarily addressing the male-relational issues in this book.
2. The issue of women and their emotional needs does not necessarily apply to all women. There are exceptions. Some women are fine and don't need tons of emotional affirmation.
3. As a marriage counselor, I recognize that a man's failures in the emotional-connection department may not be rooted in any fault of the man. It may be that his wife has erected emotional walls, or there is a place of personal woundedness infecting her heart. She may be an emotional "bucket with holes," so that no matter what you do, it isn't enough. Also, a woman who controls or micromanages her husband is sabotaging her source of intimacy by driving her husband to withdraw his emotional connecting.

4. Although I use my personal journey and experiences as examples of a journey to understand intimacy, I don't expect anyone to be like me, or like Ruthie and me. But, if the shoe fits, wear it.

Things Women Say

Things women say that men might want to give attention to.

- When I am away for a significant length of time, I always keep in contact with him, but when he is away, I hardly ever hear from him. He thinks I am insecure and doesn't like it when I tell him I need to hear from him more.
- You'd think that giving compliments and "thank yous" would be common to a man who thinks of himself as a fine Christian, but it is a rare occasion that I get anything more than modest recognition.
- I used to feel as if I were being selfish and prideful by expecting my husband to care about my feelings. Thanks to some great Christian books and a couple of great mentors, I woke up to realize that I was not being selfish at all. I was expecting things to be the way God made things to be. Marriage doesn't have to be touchy-feely all the time, but if a marriage is going to work well, both spouses need to be fulfilled in their own way, and I'm not. I know now that emotional endearments are vital to marriage and part of the romantic environment that I need and am supposed to have!
- My husband has a great heart. It's just that he never had

emotional intimacy modeled. He has no idea what it looks like and doesn't understand me when I try to tell him about my need for his warmth, affirmation, affection, and tender love.

- I read in a marriage book: "A woman needs a man to let her into his life and heart." He does not understand that. I feel like I had to strive to get inside. So after so many years, I just gave up.
- I've heard that a complete man is like Jesus, both steel and velvet. My husband is all steel. Oh, there are traces of velvet, but the scale is tipped almost the whole way on the steel side. Unfortunately, because of this, I suffer.
- When we're in a group discussion with friends, he will talk, give his opinions, tell his stories, but he never, ever says, "Honey, what do you think?" He just assumes I don't care to be involved in the discussion. That sucks. I used to think that was acceptable, but no more. Also, I wish I heard all his opinions when it's just him and me, but he doesn't open up to me that way. What wife wouldn't feel devalued?
- He expects me to understand his sexual DNA, but he doesn't make an effort to learn mine. I do the act, but my heart is not in it. He gets offended because of my lack of enthusiasm, but he won't listen to my WHY. It's a one-way street, and I despise it.

CHAPTER 6

What I Prayed over Mikah and the Other Guys

Several pages ago I told you that I prayed over the guys who came forward at the men's retreat who were having difficulty connecting with their wives. Here is the gist with some expanded comments for added clarity:

"Guys, we are all called to cover and protect the heart of our God-given spouse. I know how to meet Ruthie's emotional needs because she taught me, and I taught her about mine. But I learned something about women that I teach now all the time: women are attracted to security and strength. They want to be secure knowing that the one they made the vow to is committed to God's best for both them and their family. A woman is also drawn to strength—not physical, muscular strength, or I'd have women following me around everywhere (I got a good, satisfying laugh out of that comment, and then proceeded)—but women are attracted to strength of character. Strength means that you are courageous to do what is right in the face of opposition. Strength means that you will not let yourself be controlled by frail or carnal passions. Strength means that you will hear her, support her, and love her in the way she needs (not always "wants") to be loved."

I went on to say, "Men, it is okay to be weak. Actually it is necessary. No man is without weak moments. Only men in denial 'think' they are fine. Weakness is an opportunity for you to draw your wife into your heart. It is where she may discover your heart, feel 'one' with you and significant to walk with you when you are low. Men, it is okay to be weak, BUT…"

BUT…

"But, what she doesn't need is for you to be a WEAKLING. There is a vast difference between being weak (healthy) and being a weakling (unhealthy). In facing the challenges of life and family, you may not have a clue what to do (weak!). For you, though, to be indecisive, to fail to fight, to lack the courage to move forward and seek answers, to put your responsibility on her out of your own insecurity, to walk away in a conflict because you don't understand or agree with her, to sweep problems under the carpet as if they don't exist or will work themselves out, is unacceptable (weakling!). Today, we pray that each man here will rise to be the leaders God has called them to be. Lord, transform each heart here in a way that will significantly transform their marriages. Teach us strength in the midst of our weakness, as we recommit ourselves to trust you to lead us, to guide us, and to prosper our way! Amen."

Honey, What Do You Think?

Some of you reading this may say, "My wife is reasonably independent emotionally," and so some of this does not apply. That's okay. I have two challenges for you, though, in the form of questions: Is your wife actually emotionally independent or is she good at stuffing her feelings and being a "good girl?" Many women acquiesce to emotional tenacity because they don't value their own heart, or perhaps they have been rejected or wounded at some point, or even have given up. As a result, they become masters of adapting to the pain of not being emotionally fulfilled.

The next question: if your wife is actually emotionally healthy and doesn't need a lot of affection or emotional affirmation, then my question to you is whether your wife knows that you put a high value on her opinions and viewpoints. When Ruthie and I are with couples, frequently there are times we walk away feeling sad for the wife because in any discussion involving some form of outlook on life, or position on an issue, the husband doesn't pause to say the simple words, "Honey, what do you think?" Or when she does begin to share her heart, he interrupts or overrides her. You may think your wife is emotionally fulfilled because she doesn't need touched as much, affirmed as much, nurtured as much as you do. But she WILL be emotionally UNfulfilled if you do not value her perspectives, input, and wisdom. Does she feel as if her thoughts are subpar to yours? Maybe not. Perhaps you have a very whole and emotionally healthy wife. My challenge to you is, make sure!

CHAPTER 7

Joe Cocker and Willie Nelson on Intimacy

Joe Cocker got a boost by being one of the opening acts for the historic 1969 Woodstock rock festival. I'm not a Joe Cocker fan, but I've often enjoyed a YouTube video of Joe singing, "You Are So Beautiful To Me." It's a classic, simple, melodious song of a man telling his girl that she is beautiful:

I believe almost any woman needs to hear her husband regularly say, "You are so beautiful to me." I would venture to say to you, Mr. Husband, if you are not regularly or frequently telling your wife she is beautiful, she probably has a significant ache deep in her heart that rarely subsides. Said stronger—for a husband to not regularly tell his wife she is beautiful feels cold to me.

Too often, though, men who aren't expressive toward their wives, end up later in life singing another song, one released in 1982 by Willie Nelson, "Always On My Mind."

In this song, Willie laments to the love of his life that he didn't adequately express love, wasn't present when she needed him, and didn't prioritize the time a relationship demands. Then he begs for another chance. He seemingly, though, softens his neglect by assuring his lover that he was always thinking of her.

Don't live your life in a way that one day you will have to sing this song to your wife. The answer to the request, "Give me, give me one more chance," may be "NO!"

What If My Wife Isn't Beautiful?

I don't like to make strong, dogmatic statements, but I would suggest that if your wife isn't beautiful, you may need to rethink your perception of beautiful. Throughout my life, I didn't give myself a diet of pornography. Actually, it wasn't readily available back then. When I became a believer as a teenager, I began to loathe the image the world, the media, and our culture perpetuated as their definition of beautiful. Magazines presented images of beauty, then cable TV, then VCRs, then the internet, and all along the way the accompanying lust—all these in some way infiltrated the minds of men with their socially constructed definition of beautiful.

I'm not saying that if you think your wife isn't beautiful you are influenced by lust. I'm also not going to say that there is no such thing, in reality, as someone being more beautiful than someone else. What I'm going to say is that perceiving beauty is a heart issue. So, what do I mean?

Song Three and the Goodyear Blimp

Recently Ruthie and I watched a favorite movie of ours—Rodgers and Hammerstein's *Cinderella*. One of the lines from one of the songs in this classic musical is the prince singing to Cinderella, "Do I love you because you're beautiful, or are you beautiful because I love you?"

The last few times Ruthie was pregnant, she got big—real big. I joked with her that she could've worn blouses that had *Goodyear* written across her mid-section. People would see her in public and gasp—I mean, her "baby" area was humongous. But Ruthie was okay with her weight gain during pregnancy because, even with the change in her body, I would tell her, in those legendary words of Joe Cocker, "You are so beautiful to me." I still tell her she is beautiful almost every day, and probably multiple times each day. You see, I don't love Ruthie because she is beautiful, but she is beautiful because I love her. Ruthie could never be *not* beautiful to me, and therefore I promised her that ne'er a day will she not know that she is so beautiful to me.

I'm not tooting my own horn. I'm challenging you, my friend, to find the beauty that God sees in your wife, and learn to love her as she is. And may no day go by that she does not feel beautiful to you. Yes! She's got to FEEEEL it! Make her feel it so that she knows it deep down in her "knower" that you mean it!

CHAPTER 8

Me, Ruthie, and Ruthie and Me

When addressing the subject of emotional fulfillment in our marriage conferences, both Ruthie and I have our own stories that we frequently tell. There were times and seasons that I was hurting for more affection and endearment from Ruthie, and there were times and seasons she was aching for more from me. We have learned about each other's needs, and we have gotten healing from emotional voids in our hearts from our past.

How We Learned to Meet Each Other's Love Language

Two things enabled me to learn Ruthie's love language—one, she taught me about her needs, and two, I was committed to having a fulfilled wife. And the same applied to Ruthie learning my love language.

We couldn't love more the ways things are now! We daily live to make each other enriched, while being very careful not to create emotional dependencies, soul ties, or "unfulfillable" expectations for each other. It's good. It's great. It's normal.

How I came to be fulfilled in our relationship is for another article. Still, there was so much I had to learn about a woman's emotional needs in general, and Ruthie's particular needs. I have tons of stories about how I learned to meet these needs. If I told you half of them, I would bore the living daylights out of you. But I will tell you some of them.

Your Background Journey

So many of you men who are struggling, trying to understand how to tap into your wife's heart, have not had a father who connected to your heart. You may have had a mother connect to your heart, but for a man, I don't believe it imparts the knowledge of intimacy the same as when a man connects with his son's heart.

One of the basic needs a son needs to learn from his father is how to hold the heart of women. This lesson is not just for marriage, but in life. If more men had taught their sons to respect and protect women, there would be far less immorality among men—especially pornography.

Sometimes men who are suffering with an emotionally-unfulfilled wife were brought up with the idea that "emotional" is feminine. Just saying the word "intimacy" triggers in them *pink, girls, weak, sissy*—you get the point! But lacking emotional intimacy is not relationally healthy, and intimacy is not a female trait! I will not deny that unquestionably women are generally more feeling-oriented by virtue of female hormones and the wiring in their brain. Their sexual drive thrives on emotions.

So women are prone to wonder how a man can focus on sex as a physical thrill without soul and spirit connectivity.

Women have more estrogen, a hormone that regulates their emotions. Guys have more testosterone, which motivates dominance, confidence, risk-taking, and many other things. The role of estrogen in women and the role of testosterone in men seem to be conflicting in a relationship. Perhaps this is where John Gray got the title of his book *Men Are From Mars, Women Are From Venus.*

The Truth Is

Yet, the truth is, that when a man embraces, supports, and grows in understanding of a woman's particular needs, and a woman does the same for her husband, they will find that the Mars needs are not in conflict with the Venus needs—they are allies, helping both to be better people with broader perspectives.

So, guys, you're not going to talk your wife out of her emotional needs. You may convince her that she shouldn't feel the way she does (because you don't feel that way), which may shut down the whole person God designed her to be. But healthy, feminine emotional needs will not go away (*healthy* emotional needs!)

Yesterday I was leaving the house early to catch breakfast with a friend. I wrote a simple note to tack on the door: "Two hours away from you feels like forever! I love you!"

That note, along with other tiny notes I've written to

Ruthie, will exist in a prominent place for months where she reads and rereads them. Over a year ago, I wrote a note on our bathroom mirror with toothpaste: "I love my perfect wife." Honestly, for a couple of months I brushed my teeth looking through toothpaste. She kept it there. And now, months since she removed it, it stills appears in a vague background every time the bathroom mirror gets fogged.

Today, Ruthie went to a coffee shop with a close friend. The coffee shop was at the beginning of the trail where I jog. I didn't know she and her friend were going there, but I recognized the car. So, I popped in on her, just to say hi. Stuff like that is like bringing a rose home for no reason. It says to a woman, *he values me, he was thinking about me, he showed me love in front of my friend.*

I recently listened to a radio quiz. The audience was asked, "What makes the woman feel loved more than anything else?" I don't remember all the potential answers. (The husband bringing her home lingerie didn't win!) The prize went to PDA—public display of affection. That's what the women rated as best.

I've been married for over four decades. I've had time to learn some things you may not have had the time to learn. I do it well now, from Ruthie's standpoint, but I didn't always, as in the next story!

CHAPTER 9

A Massive Mistake

Giving gifts is not my language of love. So I suggested a policy that Ruthie agreed to—we would not give gifts to each other on special occasions. So we did not give each other gifts at Valentine's Day or Christmas, and so forth. After several years, Ruthie confessed to me that she really (really!) missed gifts since it IS one of her languages of love. I was slain in my soul with the thought of how selfish I had been. I immediately went out and bought her a new convertible Mustang—just kidding—no, I bought her a new, slinky nightie—no again—but I did make a decision and a proclamation to her that she would never feel that way again.

I had to discipline myself to learn how to give to Ruthie what I didn't need for my own satisfaction. I decided that certain holidays were opportunities to celebrate Ruthie. Now I always make those holidays special!

Ruthie doesn't need expensive gifts. I bring her home chai lattes all the time. I buy her unique candles. You know those special notes I talked about a few paragraphs back—early in our marriage, I would rarely write those lovey-dovey notes to Ruthie: HER writing notes to ME didn't boil my blood. So early in my marriage, I wasn't intrinsically motivated to write her many notes. But I learned that my little, special notes to her boiled her blood (and every guy wants a wife with boiling blood!).

A love language—we all have one—a love language is what makes me feel loved. I didn't say what makes me *know* that I am loved, but what makes me *feel* loved. A significant journey for every married person must be learning his/her partner's love language.

I had to learn these things. But, fellas, I was committed to learning how to hold Ruthie's heart. I wanted her fulfilled in marriage, but I was coming, in many areas, from the standpoint of an insensitive, styrofoam heart—not by choice, but mainly because I was born male.

Two More Lessons

PURSUIT: A girl wants to be pursued. Girls often play cat and mouse games, not because they are disinterested in an interested guy. They do it because they want to know if they are valuable enough to be pursued. Guess what, men, a woman's needs don't change after she gets married. I have learned through time and failures about Ruthie's need to be pursued. So, now, I am hot on Ruthie. I am on her like white on rice. Through nine kids and beyond, I always want Ruthie to know that she is worth pursuing.

LISTENING: There are different figures out there, but the one I heard is that women speak over 20,000 words a day—three times what men speak. These figures are elusive, but the basic gist is accurate. Women, in general, have a greater need to talk than men. They also need to talk to the man in their life. A necessary aspect of emotional connection is taking the time to listen. You don't (thank goodness!) have to listen to all 20,000, but you must listen to more than you are conditioned to listen to. Men who want a happy wife must learn to listen. Learn to like it. You, sir, are not going to change the fundamental way God made women.

Pastor David's Dominance

Ruthie and I were at a conference for leaders. David, a pastor I had known for several years, asked if Ruthie and I would join him and his wife, Pammie, for lunch. David talked about God a lot. But the problem was that he talked 95% of the time. The hard thing Ruthie and I observed is that he never gave preference for his wife to speak, never did he ask her what she thought, never did he turn and give eye contact to her when he was talking—simply to acknowledge she was as important to our conversation as Ruthie and I were. Oh, she didn't sit there totally quiet. She piped up now and then, but David never commented on what she said—instead, he always took the conversation back to his verbal agenda.

Not long into this conversation, Ruthie picks up on his disrespect. She then crafted a few questions to ask directly to Pammie. She did not make eye contact with David. But David still found a way to sabotage the conversation and lasso it back into his coral. David's wife obviously had adjusted to her husband's conversational narcissism and conformed to being shut down—likely a flawed dynamic in her marriage that was illegal for her to discuss.

I wish I could say that David and his wife were a rare case, but unfortunately, we experience this same dynamic on a semi-regular basis when meeting with couples. I wouldn't feel as if David and Pammie had a bad relationship, but I would assume she may have to, at times, "suck up" her need for significance in her marriage.

Do Women Talk Too Much?

Of course, women are prone to over-talk, too. In almost every point I make in this book you can find another side. I understand. I agree. Be please understand, as I mentioned earlier, that I am addressing issues from a male platform. Does that mean men become passive to the problem of a wife who may tend to talk too much? Indeed not. I've had to work through that issue with Ruthie. We must maturely deal with what is out of alignment in our marriage, wherever it is, but first, you must look at yourself in the mirror to see the reflection of your own heart.

By the way, our next book on this subject is Ruthie addressing how women can support and connect to the heart of her husband.

CHAPTER 10

My Sex Class

Did I get your attention? Is it ever fair that a guy gets his sexual needs fulfilled in marital sex, but his wife goes unfulfilled? Men who lack intimacy may struggle with a wife who doesn't enjoy sex because her sexual triggers are based on feeeeeeeling valued and loved. Failing to understand the needs of both of you may result in both of you being sexually unfulfilled.

No, I didn't take an instructional class on sex, but Ruthie and I taught each other—within the context of what is holy—what was fulfilling sexually, and what was not. We communicated about it. We were honest. We respected each other's needs and committed ourselves to meet those needs. For me, there were those times the day's duties were finished; the nine kids were in bed, and I'm thinking, let's have some frisky! But after many years of "choosing to be enthusiastic," Ruthie said, "Bruce, I need some let-down time after the kids go to bed, simply to chill."

"Oh," I said. "So be it!" In response to that, we'd watch the news, or listen to some songs, sit on the porch swing, talk about the day, or thoughts we were thinking. Ruthie didn't need lots of time to defrag, and even now that the kids are out of the home, we are still very busy people, and Ruthie loves to just chill before we head up to bed—frisky or no frisky!

Oh, I lied. I did have a sex class. In college I was taken under the wing, with a few other guys, of an instructor named Sumner Wemp. He taught me how to counsel marriages. The one thing I remember he taught us guys was, *sex at night begins with a good-bye kiss in the morning!* Your wife is not an object. Sex is a celebration of your love and excitement for each other.

Feeling vs. Knowing

In dealing with men and women who have father or mother wounds, a significant differentiation is feeling loved versus knowing you're loved. A child needs to feel he or she is loved. It may be easy to know you are loved, as in, my dad provided for us, my parents took us on vacations or my mom made sure we had what we needed.

But did you feel loved?

So often, this is when the tears roll, and the answer emerges through an intermittent sob of pain—"No. I never felt loved. My dad (or mom) never cared for my heart."

Guys, a wife is just like that—she needs to know she is loved, but she also needs to feel loved by you—all the time, every day, all the way. I believe this is what God desires for marriages.

What I am addressing is about two becoming one—something that is as much male as it is female. It is called going to the heart. But what does that mean?

Going to the Heart

Going to the heart is learning to be like Jesus. Women need their hubbies to talk about how they feel, what they like, what they need, and go to issues of the heart, way beyond the surface. For many men, going to the heart may be synonymous with going to Jupiter, but God gave the woman to the man to teach HIM to be more like Jesus, and He gave the man to the woman for the same reason. A husband who only lives on the surface with his wife may have to live with an eight-cylinder wife who exists on only two—short-changing both of them.

Russell Crowe and Marriage

So, I recently rewatched *Robin Hood* with Russell Crowe. I love the scene where he confronts the rebellious king. I adapted this quote to apply to your marriage.

"The laws of this land enslave people to its king—a king who demands loyalty but offers nothing [or little] in return… Empower every man [your wife], and you will gain strength."

The rest of the discourse is brilliant. The truth is, set your wife free, be wind to her back, encourage her to be everything she can be, and you, my friend, will gain strength! And I trust she will do this for you, too!

A few tips of things I learned in our four-plus decades of marriage:

- When I am talking to others, whether I am teaching or in a group chat, I don't primarily refer to Ruthie as "my wife" when I speak or write about her—she is *Ruthie.*

- When I am in a group talking to others—say at a restaurant or in the lobby after church—I make eye contact with the others…AND RUTHIE TOO.
- I always (almost) wait for Ruthie to walk ahead of me no matter where we are walking.
- I don't always open the car door for Ruthie, but I do a lot, and definitely do when we are on a date.
- Did I say this before? She is always the most important person when we're in a crowd.
- When I haven't seen her for any length of time, I greet her with a smile and a big hug.
- Enough! I don't want this to be about Ruthie and me, but I do want to offer practical wisdom for any of you who, even after reading this, are still a bit clueless.

Bucket with Holes

I am well aware that many women are emotionally wounded, in some senses quite differently than men. This is due to the need a woman has for a father's heart connection, which may have been denied her. When a woman is wounded, she can react by being controlling, emotionally dependent, insecure, self-protective. She may have a victim mentality and/or a spirit of rejection, which results in an emotional bucket filled with holes—no matter how much you pour into it, it is not enough.

In a situation such as this, a husband can partner with God to bring healing to his wife. I have been a key to much of the healing that Ruthie has encountered throughout her life. We walked through several places where, no matter what I did, it was not enough. But today Ruthie is a testimony of God's ability to heal the wounded, or the shut-down heart. In this arena, husbands need patience, relentless love, and abiding care to bear a cross while walking through his wife's emotional healing.

What's Cleaving Have to Do with This?

Genesis 2:24 says, "Therefore shall a man leave his father and his mother, and shall cleave unto his wife: and they shall be one flesh." The word cleave in this passage means to *stick to like glue.* As I looked up the Hebrew word, I noticed that the same word is used when God commands his people to cleave to Him. "That you may love the Lord your God, that you may obey His voice, and that you may cleave to Him" (Deuteronomy 30:20).

It is notable that God commands the man to cleave to his wife, not the reverse. I don't pretend to know exactly why, but I guess that the man is the pursuer and provides strength in a relationship. Perhaps most women don't need to be told to cleave to her husband. She will—if he cleaves to her. The point, though, is that men are to cleave to their wives, and there is no way to do that without the husband initiating emotional connecting.

CHAPTER 11

Exclusivity: Something Men Must Understand about Women

There is a significant characteristic of a woman that you, sir, must respect that will enable you to be a whiz at emotional connecting. That trait is her intrinsic need for exclusivity—a wife needs to know she is exclusive to you. That means that your wife is at the top of your priority list. She is the MOST special. When a man gives to others, or to other things, the time and emotion that belong to her, she will not be happy. A pastor I knew was great at showing compassion, caring, listening, and being sensitive to the women he pastored, but his wife got the leftovers—if there were any. In his professional role, he was very connecting, but in his personal, everyday mode of operandi, where he was needed most, he was passive.

I made that mistake! Not that I gave Ruthie's affection to women, but as a pastor I was diligent in meeting the needs of those I shepherded. One day Ruthie came to me and said, "Everyone in the church has a pastor...except me." Ouch! I didn't understand at first. Then it dawned on me. In my professional role, I took care of, as a matter of responsibility, the people I pastored but attended to Ruthie's spiritual needs off the clock, as if she weren't as important as the others. The lightbulb that clicked on in my brain was that meeting the needs of my wife, as a pastor, is MORE important than meeting anybody else's. Never again did Ruthie receive leftovers. But, still, I had to learn this!

A loved woman doesn't demand a huge amount of your time, but if she knows she is cared for, exclusive, and feels satisfied and embraced, she will joyfully let her man fulfill the responsibilities he needs to fulfill in his duties of life.

In order for you to understand this vital ingredient to the process of emotional connecting, both Ruthie and I will tell you a story:

Ruthie's Comments: A notable incident happened around the third year of our marriage. Bruce was a youth leader, helping to host a weekend youth retreat along with a few other leaders from our church. Our baby girl and I went along. God was touching many of the teens. But there was one particular girl Bruce made sure he didn't neglect. She was unchurched and new to the things of God—and, did I mention, she was attractive. He went out of his way to make sure he met her spiritual needs. Then one evening, late, a friend of hers came to our room and said she needed prayer, so I stayed in the room with the baby while Bruce went, counseled and prayed with this hurting young lady. When the leaders got together to pray on the last day, Bruce gave a brief testimony about how enthused he was for what God was doing in this girl's life.

I trusted Bruce fully. But this young lady, only seven or eight years younger than Bruce, was getting a full dose of emotional support from my husband. So, imagine the mental gymnastics I went through. The attention Bruce gave this girl sliced my heart, not because I didn't get MY emotional attention, but because something didn't feel exclusive. I went back and forth between beating myself up for feeling selfish and jealous, but I was also feeling violated.

Bruce: So, on the way home from the retreat, Ruthie gently explained the emotional trespass she felt with my ministry to this attractive young lady. Hearing what Ruthie said sliced my heart because there was nothing in my heart that was attracted to this girl. The talk continued after we got home. I remember that our discussion was generally peaceful, but there was indeed a wall between Ruthie's heart and mine. The more we talked, the more I realized that helping and praying for this girl wasn't the issue—the issue was my passion for it. I had crossed a boundary line for the first time in our marriage, which became my first lesson on a foundational need of a wife—exclusivity.

Before we finished our discussion, I resolved within my heart that, by God's grace, Ruthie would never, ever, feel the way she did at that retreat again. Now, over forty years later, I am writing this sitting beside Ruthie, being affirmed that a violation of exclusivity never happened again. I have prayed for and ministered to many women. We have had very close female friends, and I have given fatherly hugs to women and girls who needed it. But in all my professional and personal involvements with women, I have been careful to respect the boundaries of honor and my exclusive covenant with Ruthie.

I don't have a pattern of talking heart-to-heart to women in casual settings without Ruthie present, especially about their problems. You'll not see me at a restaurant having lunch with someone I work with, without Ruthie. I give compliments to women, but I don't give compliments to women which may fill an unfulfilled need in their soul. I give fatherly warmth to women, appropriate hugs, encouragements of all kinds, and, as a leader, pastor, or friend, I let women know I care about them.

Ruthie: There is something emotionally triumphant in me to be that "exclusive one" to Bruce. It empowers me to be me when I feel exclusive. Don't get the wrong idea—exclusiveness is not possessiveness. Many women can be jealous, clingy, and overprotective—creating a self-centered cage for their husbands. Healthy exclusivity is a celebration of oneness!

This is why pornography is so violating! Pornography is always wrong for both men and women—it is not just a male problem, but allow me to speak for godly women—a husband who feeds on pornography will assault the value of his wife and profanes the covenant he made to her. She will not feel exclusive, she will not feel adequate, she will not feel loved, she will be tempted to "measure up" to an unreachable image, and she will be unable to give true intimacy and respect to her husband.

Bruce: I know Ruthie is neither a jealous person, nor possessive. She is not a needy "bucket with holes." So whenever she communicates that she might be uncomfortable with a situation that I am in, one that might feel non-exclusive—there is no discussion, case closed—I adjust to her comfort level. As a result, Ruthie lavishes me with freedom and trust, no matter where I am or what I am doing.

Ruthie: Here are more thoughts about what exclusivity means to a woman:

- She is affirmed for her total beauty and appreciated for all she does.
- She never has to strive or compete for her husband's attention.
- She is "enough" for her man—he doesn't make her feel like plan B or leftovers.
- When any situation arises, she is the first one her husband thinks of or takes care of.
- A wife doesn't have to be the center of attention. She only needs to know that it matters to her husband that she is there.
- She is the only one who gets her husband's primary affection.

Exclusivity Beyond Women

Ruthie: Exclusivity is an issue when husbands are giving too much time and energy to work, video games, sports, and other involvements to the detriment of his wife and family. Notice I didn't say "when men are giving time." I said "too much time." However, many women over-inject their need for exclusivity and shut down a husband's creative, "wild-at-heart" motivations. Men need to be careful if hunting, for example, is hurting the family, but from the other side, I tell women: you can take the man out of the forest, but you can't take the forest out of the man! Women, why not get behind him and encourage his hunting, or any other legitimate hobby? I'm not saying to accept something that may be out of alignment, but sacrifice a bit of your time with your husband so he can enjoy fulfilling those dreams in his heart.

Aren't Men Exclusive, Too?

Bruce: Both men and women possess a need to be exclusive to their lover, but I believe, due to a woman's emotional makeup and her intrinsic emotional needs, her need for exclusivity has a broader scope than a man's. Also, though we see violations go both ways, we see women crying out for exclusivity far more than men, perhaps because women, out of their own need, are more likely to give exclusivity to a man. As a result, women seem to understand exclusivity in a way men often don't.

Ruthie: Bruce travels a lot, but I always know that I am on his mind—no matter where he is or how busy his schedule is. When he is away he takes time to call me and let me know that he is thinking about me. If he is in meetings all day, he'll text me during a bathroom break—not because he has to, but because we love connecting. The culture of our marriage is nurturing our romance, respecting our covenant, and keeping the Lord as the bond between us.

Back to Bruce: Guys, What may happen when you start emotionally connecting?

Building trust with your wife in the emotional arena may not happen overnight. Depending on the severity of emotional neglect you have inflicted, you may have some challenges to bring your relationship with your wife to a healthy place. You must be willing to give this journey the time it needs, and the time she needs. Apologies eventually will be needed—you taking responsibility for self-centeredness, control, neglect, or perhaps your cluelessness about how God designed women. Apologies will be needed for specific incidences where you may have done or not done something that may have wounded her. For example, if you went away on a four-day business trip and only called her once during those four days, instead of what you should have done—call her once or more every day. (The times you need to be MOST diligent about emotionally connecting with her is when the two of you are away from each other.) Ask forgiveness. Or if you failed to tell your wife regularly how beautiful she is, or that you love her. Ask forgiveness.

Your apologies may be needed at the beginning. They may bring fast healing, but then again, they may be received only after you have re-established trust again. The best illustration I've seen about the process of a man building trust with his wife is the movie *Fireproof* by Sherwood Pictures. Watch it, or watch it again!

CHAPTER 12

A Word to Women on Shutting Down Hubby

I would be naive if I thought this book was only going to be read by men! The reality is that more women than men may read this book…maybe—women who need validation for their own feelings and support for their hearts. So, for you women reading this, I asked Ruthie to illuminate some things wives do that put emotional distance between them and their husbands.

From Ruthie

For years, in the counseling room, in our pastoral relationships, or with friends, I've heard women complain over and over again, "My husband doesn't fulfill me emotionally." Though, as you have just read on the previous pages of this book, many men need enlightened about the needs of a woman. But let me take a few paragraphs to enlighten you wives about ways you may be amplifying the problem.

Over-talking: This was addressed earlier in this book, but I need to emphasize it. Quite often Bruce and I are with couples watching her dominating him in conversation—interrupting his sentences, answering questions without giving him a chance to respond—dishonoring her husband with an unattractive amount of words. When I see this, I can usually guess there are other control issues regarding how she relates to her husband.

Nagging: Traditional jokes about marriage always emphasize the nagging wife. There may be things you legitimately need to be persistent about, but if you are a nagging wife, you likely will suffer from some level of an emotionally detached husband.

Micromanaging: The same has to do with micromanaging, which is a form of nagging: Park over there! Do you really want to eat that much ice cream? I think you need to call your boss and blah, blah, blah. He turns on the heater and you turn it off, and on and on. Wife, you may think you are helping your husband, but in your desire to help him, realize that no matter how you justify it, micromanaging will never bless your husband. He may do what you say, but he's simultaneously stuffing resentment toward you, which will create a detachment between you.

My Way or the Highway: Many wives push away their husbands by being overly opinionated or over-structured—you have over-defined ways YOU like things to be done or strong opinions which keep your husband's opinions or preferences on the outside. Does your husband think you give him lip service—pretending to agree with some of his directives and suggestions, but then you do the opposite?

Mothering: Must I mention mothering? Your husband doesn't need another mother—even if he wants one. If you want an emotionally dull husband, mother him: Did you brush your teeth? I think you should wear that other pair of shoes! Let's sit here instead of there. Are you watching your weight?

Sexual Dullness: The sexual relationship is vital to a man. Bruce taught me that mature men need and want more than the act. I have learned to emotionalize Bruce in our sexual intimacy. This means that I make him feel loved, valued, and excited about our sex. I realize that if your husband doesn't treat you with sexual respect and value your sexual needs, this may be difficult, but my challenge to you is to choose to be enthusiastic about sex, and there's a good chance you'll see your husband drawing close to you.

Feminizing: Your husband is male. He has more testosterone than you. Don't feminize your husband or create a household culture that makes being male unsafe. Bruce says:

Touché to Feminization!

I'm against the putrid feminization of men—be touchy-feely, be soft, never burp, give up all your spiky, male nature. No! Early in our marriage Ruthie tried to make me socially palatable, proper in every situation, never brash. That was a problem! But another problem was that I took it. I didn't know better. Gradually we communicated about it. It took time. Now I always thank Ruthie for letting me be male. (She still doesn't like me burping!)

I'm not saying it is good or godly, but a man resists being

controlled. It is challenging for a man to pour out his emotions in the face of feeling violated or controlled.

CHAPTER 13

Would You Rather I Be Boring?

I was watching a movie. On the wall in one scene was a sign that said, "May I be the reason someone smiles *today!*" I told Ruthie, "That's a motto that describes my heart!"

Having fun with somebody makes them feel valued. My humor is bizarre. I break rules. I take risks. Now and then in bed at night, I catch myself thinking, *Dang, I shouldn't have said that*, as I reminisce over the day's jesting, but that's all part of it! I have fun with servers in restaurants, strangers in the isles of Walmart, in the doctor's office, and at some point in every public lesson I teach on any subject. But the place I value humor the most is at home. Ruthie and I laugh every day—or should I say, all the time. I have my "male" humor, and she embellishes it with her safer style. We have our secret archive of irreverent humor that I wouldn't share with you if you threatened to poison my gizzard, or torture me by taking me Christmas caroling. My kids don't laugh at all my jokes anymore as the jokes have transitioned from dad jokes to grandfather jokes.

May I be the reason someone smiles today! But may I be the reason Ruthie smiles today! Not too long ago Ruthie and

I were talking to a wonderful woman who is going through a divorce because of an unfaithful husband. I asked her if her husband ever initiated fun with her. Her answer was, "Not for the last five or ten years." Ouch! So sad. Laughter is such an amazing emotional stabilizer, healer, and bonding agent.

You certainly don't have to be like me—obnoxious and purely weird at regular intervals. Still, it would do you good to begin establishing a habit of keeping the smile in your marriage every single day.

So when my kids—or Ruthie—groan at one of my jokes—like a joke I use publicly that they've heard thousands of times (but still gets a crowd giggle), I can be heard to say (and I'm sure it will be on my gravestone), "Would you rather I be boring?" Enjoy a little poem I wrote:

I'm Bizarre

I'm a little bizarre
(well, more than little,
by far)

Often I'm a bit weird
but nothing
to be feared

unless
of course
I'm strange

while I'm
within your
range

while you're behaving
formal
you'll notice I'm
abnormal

At times I'm
unaware
that I
am acting
rare

you may inquire
why God
made anyone
so odd

But truthfully on my behalf
I'm just trying to make you
laugh!

CHAPTER 14

The Value of Cows and Women

I hope I've presented to you a balanced teaching, one you will have to sort through which part of it applies to your marriage, your life, and your wife. As I wrote at the beginning of this book, the content won't be applicable to all women, all marriages. But if this does apply in your case, I trust you will make a solid commitment to invest more of who you are into your covenant partner. God bless you as you do!

Oh, but before I close this teaching, I have a question for you…

How Many Cows Is Your Wife Worth?

As a creative writer, I know the feeling when you run into a story or an article that inside you say, *Dang, I wish I had written that!* That's what I feel about the incredible short story "The Eight-Cow Wife" by Patricia McGerr. The story centers around the mystery of Johnny Lingo, who was known to be the sharpest trader in the region.

The story opens with Shenkin talking to a visitor to his island, Kiniwata, about Johnny Lingo, on the veranda of his guest house. After explaining to the guest how shrewd Johnny was, he told him that nobody on the island could figure out why such an amazing trader came to their island and paid eight cows for a wife—Sarita. Ha, Sarita's father would have gladly taken one cow for her, as homely as she was. Shenkin told the guest that it would be kindness to call her plain—no endowments, walked with her head down, and scared of her own shadow. So why did Johnny pay more cows for Sarita than had ever been paid for any woman on the island? Mystery!

The conversation continues, but the guest decides that he will travel to the island of Nurabandi to uncover why this Johnny Lingo guy would pay so much for an undesirable woman to be his wife, when he could've secured her for a single cow.

When the guest arrived at the island, he visited Johnny. While there, a woman came out and put a bowl of blossoms on a table and then exited the room. The guest thought she was the most beautiful woman he had ever seen—"ethereal loveliness." Surely this was not the Sarita Shenkin described. But if not, then who was this woman, and where was Sarita?

After a fun conversation the truth emerged—the mystery was solved. Johnny was as sharp as everybody thought he was. The lovely woman was Sarita, and the reason Johnny paid eight cows for her was, "I wanted an eight-cow wife."[1]

No story could ever express more accurately what I've just written to you in just a hair more than 11,500 words. Call it dessert to the main meal—but never forget the amazing truth this short story conveys! May you and your wife discover a deeper and more intimate relationship that enables both of you to enjoy the magnificent glory of marriage!

1 "The Eight-Cow Wife", by Patricia McGerr, (Adapted and edited from its original appearance in *Reader's Digest*, February 1988, pp138-141)

ADDENDUM

Summarizing This Book in Rhyme

I present a poem I wrote for Ruthie that I mean with all my heart. Honestly, this poem expresses what this whole book is about. Read it with all your heart!

You're a Princess

Every day of
your life
every moment
within
no matter what is,
or ever
has been

Without ere a doubt
I want you to see
that you're
a magnificent
princess
to me.

When you wake
in the morn,
I want you to know
and then through the day
to feel it
overflow
the love that reveals,
you're the best
of the best
stars above others,
perfect and
blessed!

not ever a moment,
that you do not feel,
celebrated
cherished
far beyond
my ideal

God forbid you would
ever conceive,
a thought
that would
cause you
to fail to
receive,
the jewels and
the splendor
God placed
on your crown,
that no demon
in Hell
could ever
shut down

But I have decided
I've made it my plan
as much as is possible
as much as I
can,
I'll treat you like
royalty
I'll lavish your
soul
I'll fill you up,
fill you up
fill you up
full

It won't be by me
If you are unsure
about your amazingness
about your
allure
oh,
it won't be by me
if you forget your appeal,
I won't be to blame,
if you don't feel
the feel,

of being a
glorious princess
in lace,
of having
the countenance
of God on your face

you'll never be hurting
to hear me declare,
that you're gorgeous,
alluring,
none
can compare

you're beautiful
charming
addictive
divine,
I'll say and repeat it,
I'm thrilled
that you're mine

for I will remind you
I'll never be shy
you'll hear
me express it
every day till
we die,
that you are
majestic
a princess of worth,
like no one
I've ever heard of
on earth.

nothing more could be better,
this I know through and through,
than the privilege of being
married…
to you.

Other books by Bruce Lengeman

Kingdom Culture

Uncovering the Heart of What Empowers Teams

Create a culture in your business, your church, and your family that values people, and operates with efficiency and productivity. This book will save you countless hours putting out crisis fires, morale issues, and stagnancy.

To Kill A Lion

Transforming Your Life through Sexual Freedom

This book answers the question many men ask about sexual lust: *I know it's wrong, but why can't I stop?* It takes you into the control room of your heart, beyond the surface and helps you discover what is driving the drive, how to find freedom, and how to value your God-given sexuality.

You've Been Tweeked

The Secret of Overcoming Everything

One businessman wrote, "It's a must for anyone who wants to go anywhere." *You've Been Tweeked* is an illuminating and uncanny fable that uncovers why some people succeed and others don't—in marriage, in business, in life.

God, Do You Play?

A full-color book for children

Teaches children in a fun way that God is with them all the time. One parent reported, "After two years of reading *God, Do You Play?* it is still my daughter's favorite book!"

About Bruce Lengeman

Bruce Lengeman has been in ministry since 1976 when he graduated from college with a degree in pastoral studies. He has served in ministry as a youth leader, young adult leader, and other aspects of ministry. After six years as a professional counselor, he planted a church in 1991 where he was the senior pastor for over nine years. After pastoring, he focused on business consulting and was active doing business conferences and other seminars, often team-teaching with Ruthie, his wife. Bruce served as the pastor of ACTS Covenant Fellowship in Lancaster, PA, for five years. He now oversees this congregation as well as a recent church plant from ACTS. Bruce and Ruthie are actively working with primary leaders and doing a variety of seminars and conferences in the US and overseas. One of his primary focuses is calling men to be what they were designed by God to be.

Bruce and Ruthie have nine children and 20 grandchildren and counting.

Contact information

Contact Bruce and Ruthie for speaking engagements at:
Website: BruceLengeman.com
Facebook: Bruce Lengeman or Bruce Lengeman Ministries.